Blood

Written by Martin Bolod
Illustrated by Alan Baker and Sholto Walker

Contents

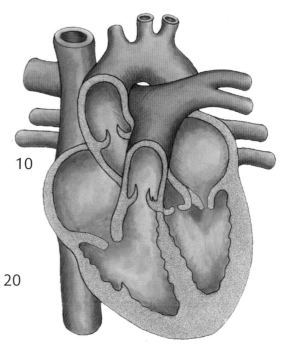

Collins

Blood is good!

If you've ever cut yourself or had a nose bleed, you'll know that your body is filled with a red liquid – blood!

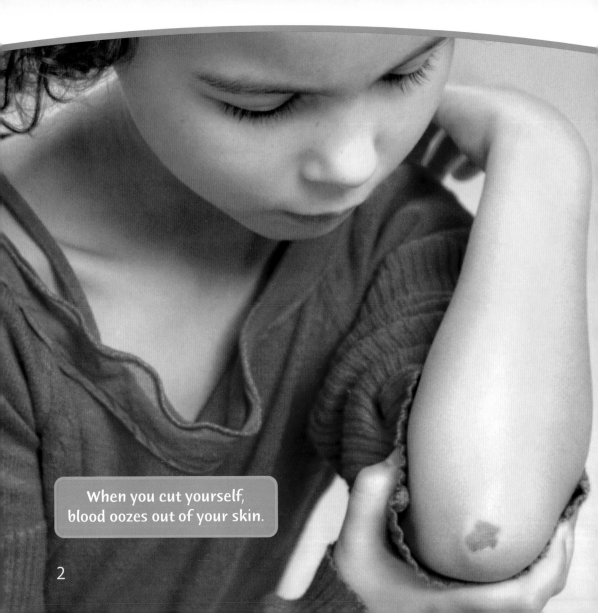

When you cut yourself, blood oozes out of your skin.

A newborn baby has enough blood in its body to fill
a mug. An adult has about five litres of blood.
That's enough to fill 15 mugs!

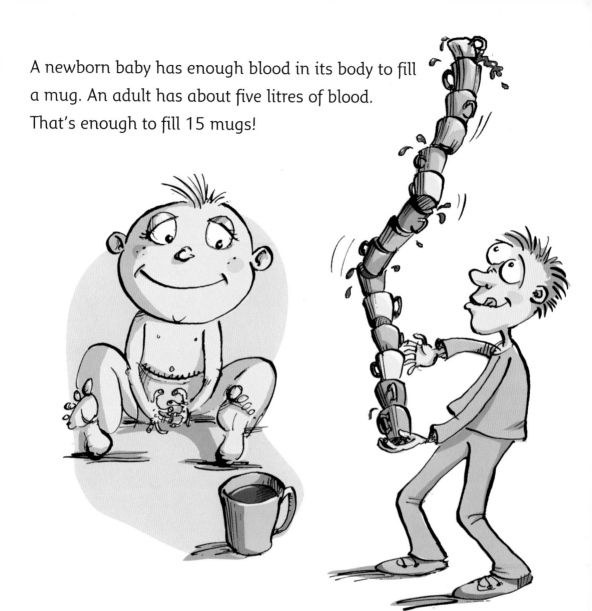

Blood does lots of very important jobs in your body.
It keeps you alive! Blood gives your body the things it needs
and takes away the things it doesn't. It also helps to fight
germs and illnesses.

Cells

Each drop of blood in your body has millions of tiny cells in it. These blood cells float in a watery liquid.

There are two different kinds of blood cells: red blood cells and white blood cells.

a red blood cell

a white blood cell

The little round blobs here are your blood cells. This is how your blood would look if you could see the cells 1,000 times bigger than they actually are.

Blood cells are made inside your bones. Your bones are very hard on the outside, but inside they are hollow and filled with a soft jelly. Blood cells are made in this jelly and then sent all around your body.

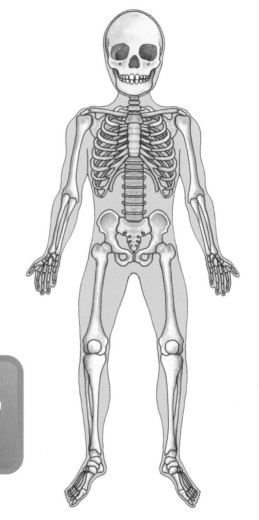

Fact

Each blood cell lives for about four months and a healthy person makes millions of new blood cells in their bones every day.

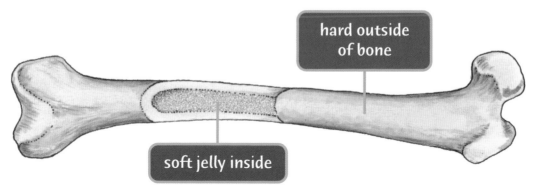

hard outside of bone

soft jelly inside

5

Red blood cells

Most of the cells in your blood are red blood cells. A single drop of blood contains about 300 million of them.

Red blood cells are disc shaped, but are thicker at the edges than at the centre – a bit like a pizza!

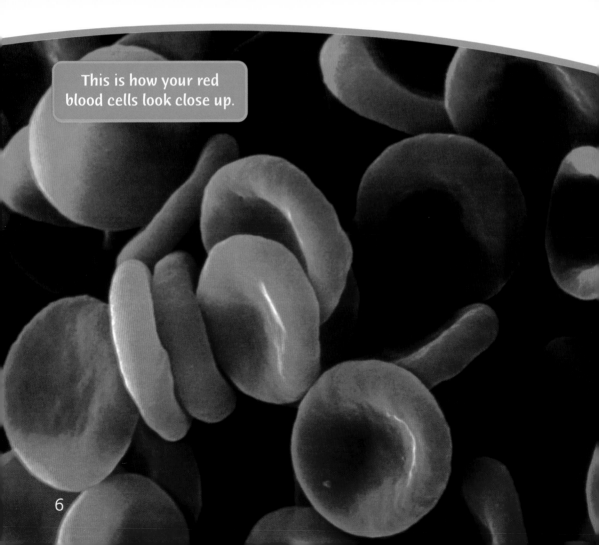

This is how your red blood cells look close up.

Have you ever tried to hold your breath? You can't do it for long, because everyone needs to breathe air every minute of the day and night. This is because air contains oxygen and our bodies need oxygen to stay alive.

The job of the red blood cells is to carry oxygen all around your body to where it is needed.

Red blood cells soak up oxygen like a sponge. Oxygen makes the cells go bright red. That's why blood is red.

White blood cells

White blood cells are larger than red blood cells, but there are not as many of them.

White blood cells look white when there are lots of them together, but if you looked at each cell closely you would see that they are different colours.

White blood cells travel around your body with red blood cells. Their job is to defend your body from germs and other things that have invaded it.

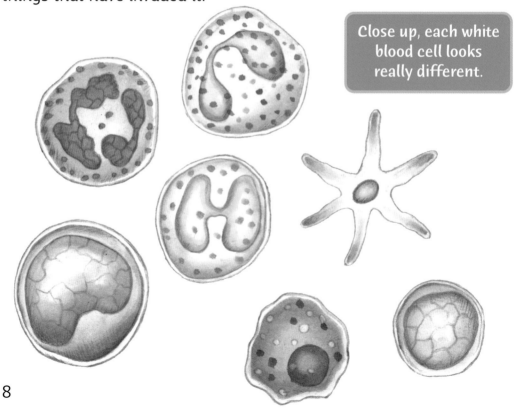

Close up, each white blood cell looks really different.

Some white blood cells hunt down invaders and fight them.

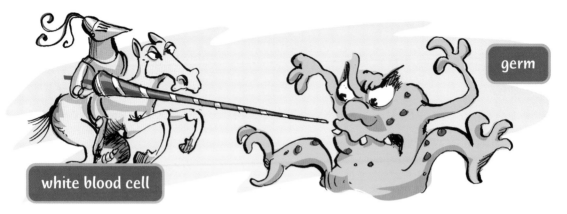

germ

white blood cell

Others change invaders into something harmless.

While others simply swallow them whole!

Travelling through blood tubes

Now you know what blood is made of. But how does it get to where your body needs it?

Blood travels around your body in tubes. The tubes branch off in many directions and go everywhere inside your body, a bit like an underground railway.

Your blood goes around the tubes in a loop. It takes about a minute for the blood to go all the way around your body and back to where it started.

Fact

If all the blood tubes in your body were joined end to end, they'd be long enough to go around the Earth twice!

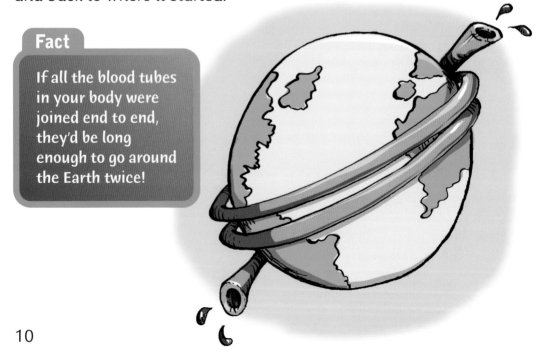

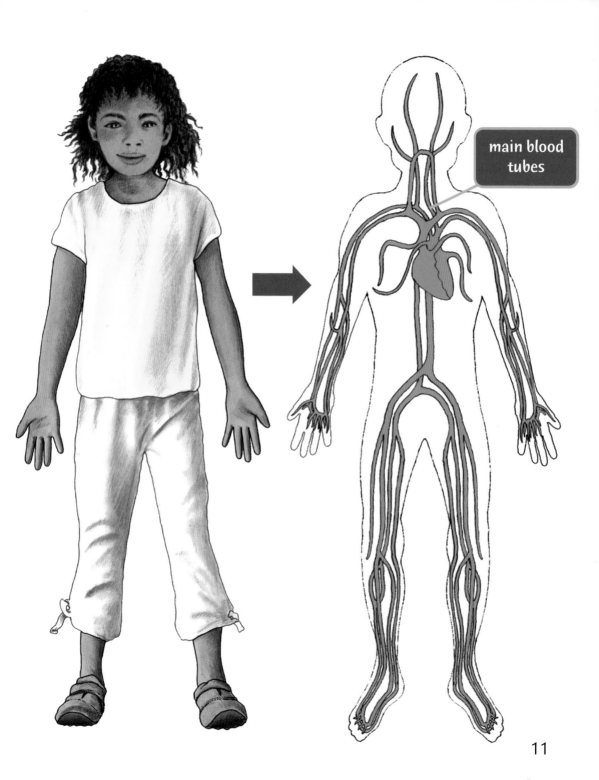

main blood
tubes

11

Let's start with your heart

As your blood travels around your body it goes through your heart. Your heart is the pump that keeps your blood moving. It's about the size of your fist and it sits in the middle of your chest, but it's tilted slightly to the left.

Your heart is behind your rib bones.

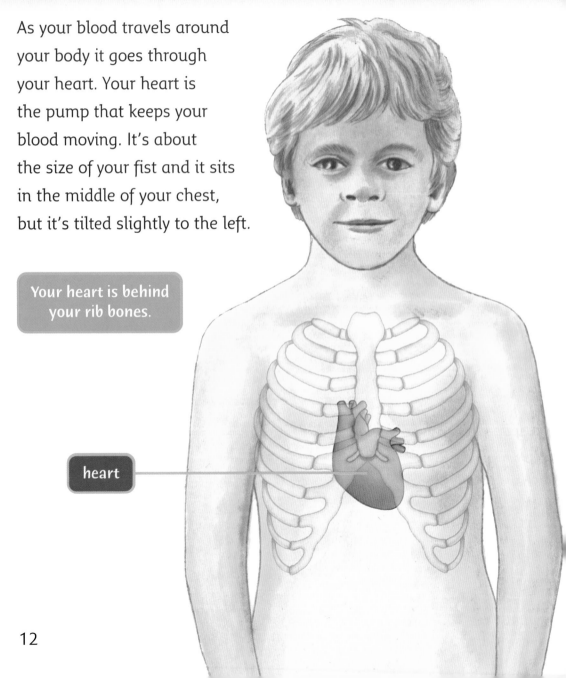

heart

Your heart is a muscle. It's one of your biggest and strongest muscles and it pumps blood around your body every moment of your life.

Your heart is hollow, a bit like a balloon, but it's filled with blood instead of air. Every time your heart "beats", the muscle tightens and blood is squeezed out, like air being squeezed out of a balloon. Then your heart relaxes and fills with blood, ready to pump again.

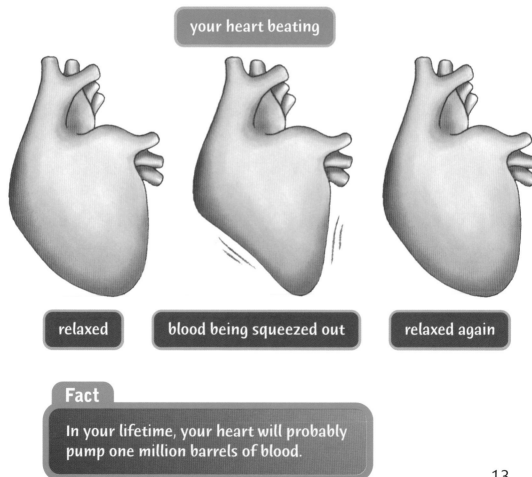

your heart beating

relaxed

blood being squeezed out

relaxed again

Fact

In your lifetime, your heart will probably pump one million barrels of blood.

13

Your heart in two parts

Your heart is divided into two main parts.

One part of your heart takes blood from your body and sends it to your lungs. The other part of your heart takes blood from your lungs and pumps it to your body.

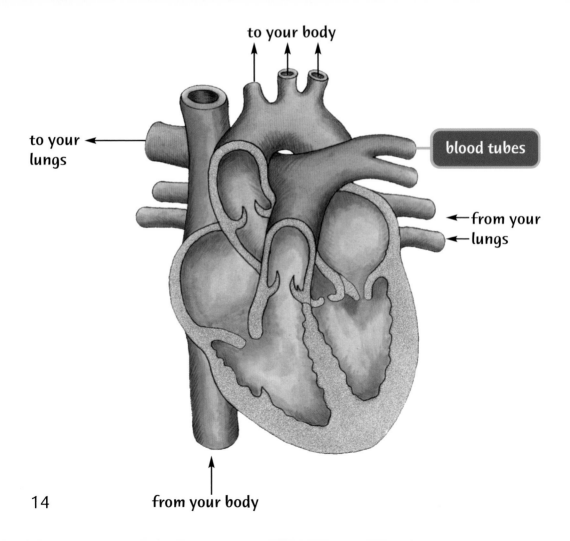

to your body

to your lungs

blood tubes

from your lungs

from your body

Your heart beats about 90 times a minute, which is about 130,000 times a day. But your heart beats faster when you're exercising – or when you're scared or excited. This is why emotions like love are said to come "from the heart".

Fact

Exercise is good for your heart because it helps to keep it healthy.

First stop, your lungs

Your heart pumps blood into tiny tubes that go through your lungs.

Your lungs are two sacks of air, which take up most of the space inside your chest. Every time you breathe in, your lungs fill with air, and every time you breathe out, they empty again.

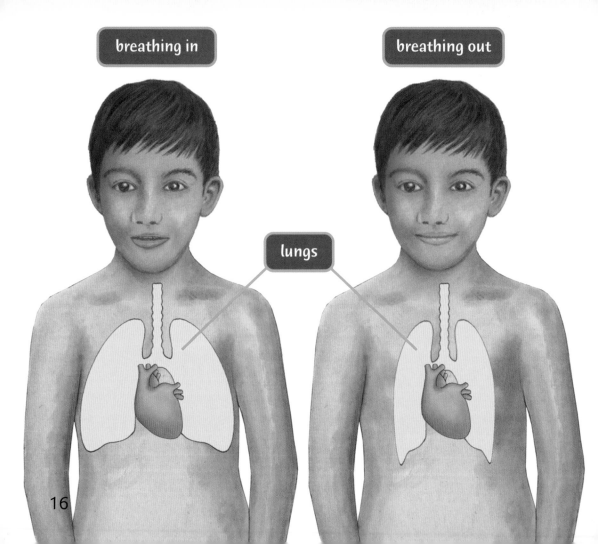

breathing in

breathing out

lungs

Blood is your body's delivery service.

As blood goes through your lungs, red blood cells pick up oxygen from the air you've breathed in. Then, when your blood has picked up its load of oxygen, it goes back to your heart, ready to be pumped around your body.

When your blood has delivered all its oxygen, it comes back to your heart, to be sent to your lungs again to collect more.

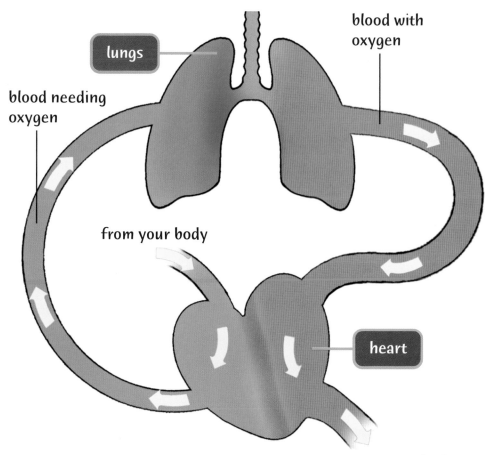

blood with oxygen

lungs

blood needing oxygen

from your body

heart

to your body

Off into your arteries

Your heart pumps the blood, loaded with oxygen, out into your arteries. Your arteries are the tubes that carry your blood to wherever it's needed in your body.

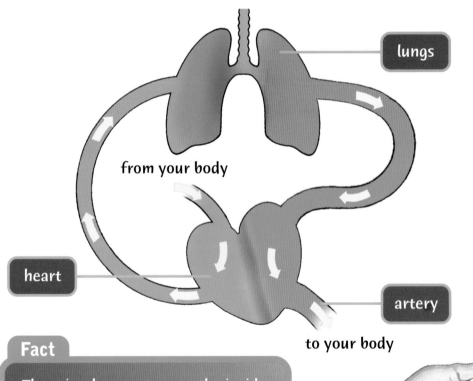

lungs

from your body

heart

artery

to your body

Fact

There is a large artery on the inside of your wrist, just below your thumb. If you put your finger on it, you should be able to feel a small beat. This is called a pulse and it is made every time your heart pumps blood.

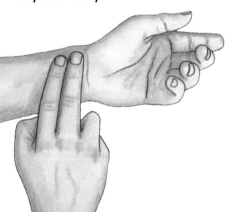

The artery that carries the blood from your heart is the biggest in your body and is about as thick as a hose pipe. This artery splits into smaller and smaller arteries that spread out inside your body like the branches of a tree.

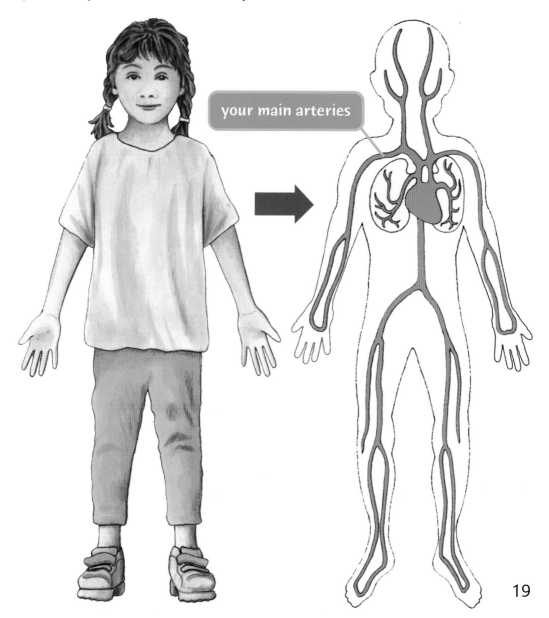

your main arteries

All change at your capillaries

Your arteries branch into smaller and smaller tubes, and your smallest tubes are called capillaries. Capillaries are everywhere in your body. This is where your blood hands over what your body needs. As the blood goes through your capillaries, the red blood cells give their oxygen to your body. Your blood also carries food and water to your body, to make it live and grow. And it carries away anything that your body doesn't want.

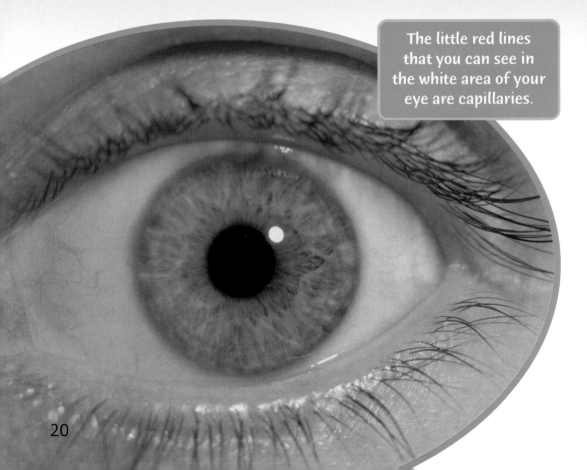

The little red lines that you can see in the white area of your eye are capillaries.

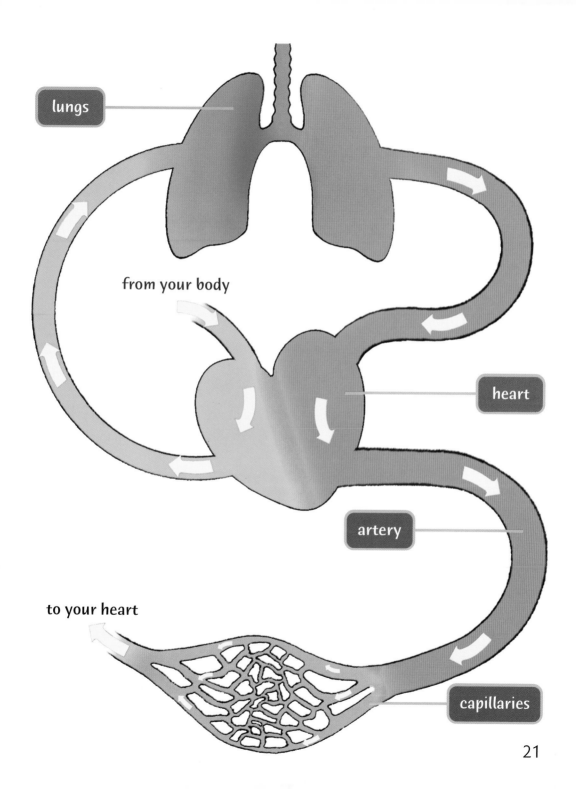

lungs

from your body

heart

artery

to your heart

capillaries

21

And back again in a vein

After your blood has given away its oxygen at the capillaries,
it has to go back to your lungs to collect more. So your capillaries
join together into larger tubes called veins. Your veins join
together into bigger and bigger veins that take blood back
to your heart. This blood is then pumped to your lungs and
the whole journey starts over again.

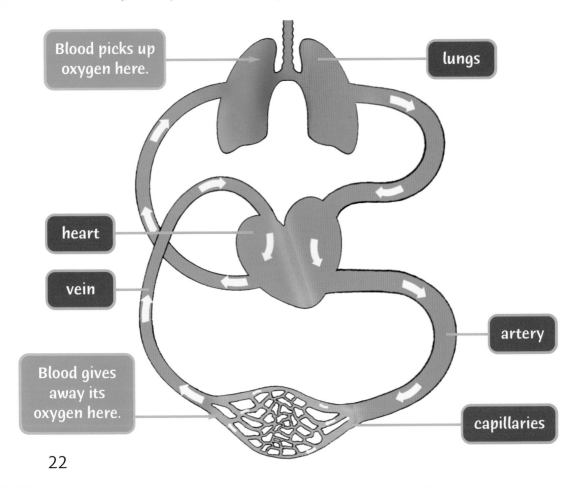

Blood picks up oxygen here.

lungs

heart

vein

Blood gives away its oxygen here.

artery

capillaries

Veins are like arteries, but there are some differences. Arteries have strong thick walls and can grow bigger if your heart is pumping lots of blood. Veins have thin walls and one-way "doors" inside them to stop the blood going backwards.

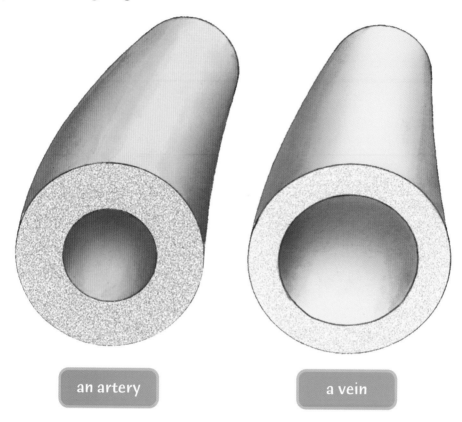

an artery

a vein

Veins and arteries are also different colours. Arteries are red, because they're filled with red blood cells that are full of oxygen. Veins look blue, because the red blood cells turn blue once they've delivered their oxygen. This blue colour makes your veins much easier to see in your skin.

Fixing a hole

If you have a cut in your skin, blood will ooze out of it –
you will bleed.

This is because the cut has made holes in your capillaries, letting
your blood leak out. Your body must fix these holes quickly before
you lose too much blood.

Your body fixes the holes by making red blood cells stick together.
The red blood cells make lumps, called clots, which plug up
the holes.

A large clot is also made on your skin, over the cut, which dries
out to become a scab. The hard scab stops germs from getting
into the cut while your skin is being repaired.

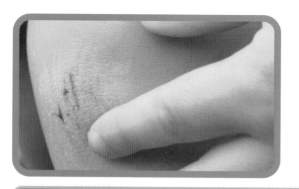 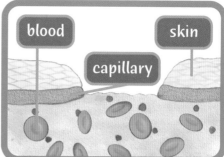

When you cut yourself, you make a hole in your capillaries.

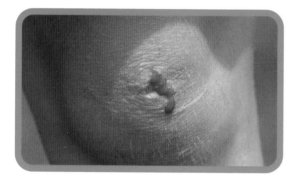 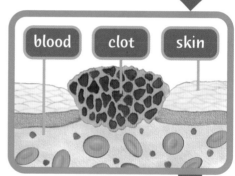

Red blood cells stick together to make a clot.

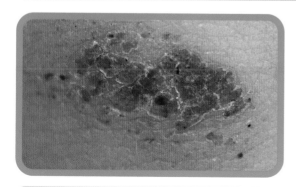 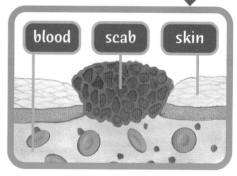

The clot plugs the hole and forms a scab.

Food, glorious food

As well as oxygen, your body needs food and water. But how does food and water get from your tummy to where your body needs it – like the tips of your fingers? The answer is that it travels in your blood!

The food you eat is broken down into tiny bits in your intestines. Your intestines are a very long, sausage-like tube in your tummy, filled with the food you've eaten.

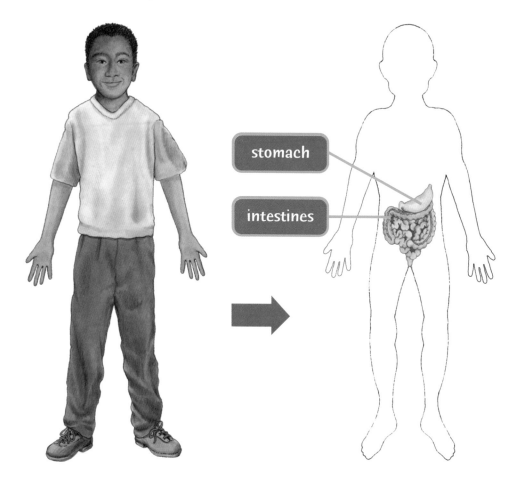

stomach

intestines

The tiny bits of food are taken from your intestines and mixed into your blood before it is pumped around your body.

Water is taken from your intestines and mixed with your blood, so that it can also be pumped all around your body.

Taking out the rubbish

All the things your body does not want, such as germs and worn-out blood cells, are carried away by your blood, too. Your body then cleans them out of your blood and gets rid of them when you go to the toilet.

So now you know what blood is made of, how it travels to everywhere in your body and the important jobs it does.

Index

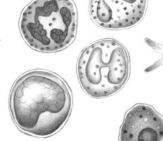

Blood in your body

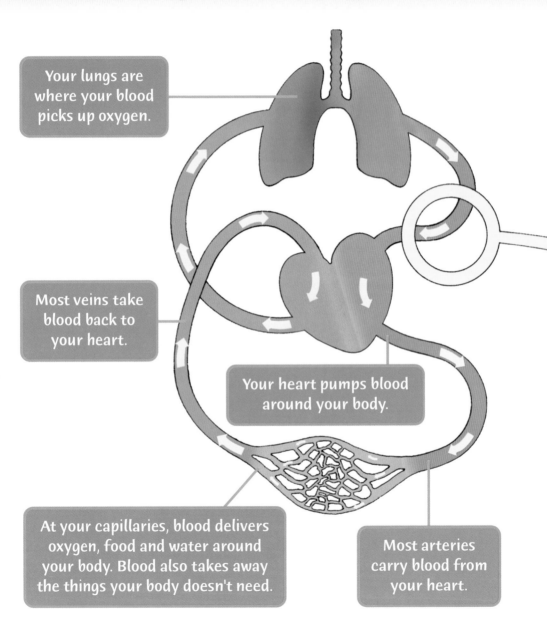

Your lungs are where your blood picks up oxygen.

Most veins take blood back to your heart.

Your heart pumps blood around your body.

At your capillaries, blood delivers oxygen, food and water around your body. Blood also takes away the things your body doesn't need.

Most arteries carry blood from your heart.

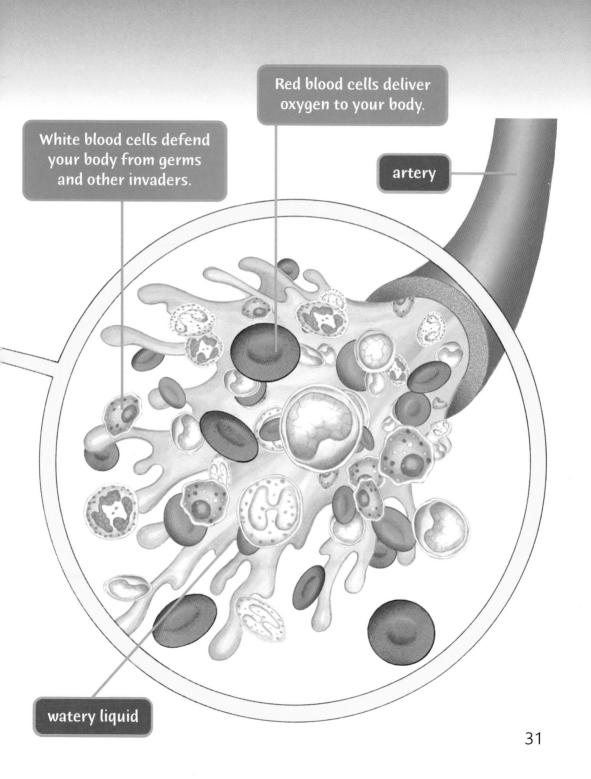

Red blood cells deliver oxygen to your body.

White blood cells defend your body from germs and other invaders.

artery

watery liquid

 Ideas for reading

Written by Clare Dowdall BA(Ed), MA(Ed)
Lecturer and Primary Literacy Consultant

Learning objectives: draw together ideas and information from across a whole text, using simple signposts in the text; explain organisational features of texts, including alphabetical order, layout, diagrams, captions, hyperlinks and bullet points; read whole books on their own, choosing and justifying selections; listen to each other's views and preferences, agree the next steps to take and identify contributions by each group member

Curriculum links: Science: Health and Growth

Interest words: white blood cells, heart, lungs, arteries, capillaries, vein, germs, bones, oxygen, invaders, muscles, pulse, carbon dioxide, clots

Word count: 1,683

Resources: large cards with interest words written on them: *heart, lungs, arteries, veins, capillaries*

Getting started

- Look at the front and back covers. Ask children to read the blurb aloud together. Ask for any ideas that children have about the jobs that blood does.

- Look at the title page. Ask children to read through the contents, writing down tricky and new words.

- Share the tricky words and revise strategies for tackling them, e.g. phonics, looking for common endings.

Reading and responding

- Read pp2–3 aloud together. Discuss the purpose of this section of the book, to introduce the subject and explain what blood is and does.

- Look at pp4–5 together. Model how to read for meaning using the captions, photographs, diagrams and fact boxes, e.g. *I wonder what this is? This box says...* etc.

- Ask children to read the book in pairs using the organisational features to help them to make meaning from the text.

- Support children to make meaning as they read by asking them questions and helping them to decode new or tricky words.